MASTERS OF DISGUISE

AMAZING ANIMAL TRICKSTERS

REBECCA L. JOHNSON

M MILLBROOK PRESS · MINNEAPOLIS

"NOW, HERE, YOU SEE, IT TAKES ALL THE RUNNING YOU CAN DO, TO KEEP IN THE SAME PLACE."

—The Red Queen, *Through the Looking-Glass* by Lewis Carroll, 1872

I am grateful to the following scientists who took time from their busy schedules to answer my questions and share their insights and experiences about the marvelous "masters of disguise" in this book: Francesca Barbero, Rohan Brooker, Aaron Corcoran, Robert Jackson, Danielle Klomp, Gustavo Londoño, Simon Pollard, Claire Spottiswoode, Phil Torres, and Anne Wignall. Where would we be without curious, dedicated people such as these researchers, who introduce us to the amazing life forms with which we share this planet? Many, many thanks!

Millbrook Press™
An imprint of Lerner Publishing Group, Inc.
241 First Avenue North
Minneapolis, MN 55401 USA

For reading levels and more information, look up this title at www.lernerbooks.com.

Main body text set in Avenir LT Std 55 Roman.
Typeface provided by Adobe Systems.

Library of Congress Cataloging-in-Publication Data

Names: Johnson, Rebecca L., author.
Title: Masters of disguise : amazing animal tricksters / Rebecca L. Johnson.
Description: Minneapolis : Millbrook Press, 2016. | Includes bibliographical references and index.
Identifiers: LCCN 2015031648| ISBN 9781512400878 (lb : alk. paper) | ISBN 9781512401059 (eb pdf : alk. paper)
Subjects: LCSH: Mimicry (Biology)—Juvenile literature. | Camouflage (Biology)—Juvenile literature.
Classification: LCC QH546 .J64 2016 | DDC 591.47/3—dc23

LC record available at http://lccn.loc.gov/2015031648

Manufactured in the United States of America
2-51665-20906-12/3/2021

CONTENTS

Introduction
THE ART OF DECEPTION

Imagine you're a spy carrying secret documents. You're aboard a train traveling deep into foreign territory. Enemy agents will be waiting at the station. And they'll be looking for you.

You adjust your wig and slip on a pair of glasses. As the train pulls into the station, you wrap a thick scarf around your neck and chin. The enemy agents are there, as expected. They're glancing back and forth between the disembarking passengers and a photo they're clutching. A photo of you.

A tough-looking agent stares right at you. Then his eyes slide past to the face of the person behind you. You walk on, smiling secretly to yourself. Your disguise worked!

In books and movies, spies often conceal their identity with clever costumes, masks, and makeup. But the most amazing

Take camouflage. That's the ability to hide by blending in with one's surroundings. Many animals are so well camouflaged that they are all but impossible to see in their natural habitat. And then there's mimicry, where an animal is disguised as something else—a rock, a thorn, a nasty stinging insect—and gains protection or some sort of advantage as a result.

The masters of disguise you'll meet in this book, however, take the art of deception to new heights. They have built on the basics of camouflage and mimicry with sounds, scents, movements, and a host of special skills. These talented tricksters are able to dupe, hoodwink, and bamboozle other animals in absolutely amazing ways.

Can you find the owl in this picture? The colors and patterns in this owl's feathers make them a near-perfect match to tree bark. The patterns also break up the outlines of the bird, which makes spotting it harder still.

Chapter 1

COAT OF MANY CORPSES

THE MASTER: Assassin bug
(*Acanthaspis petax*), a.k.a. the
Corpse Collector

THE DISGUISE: A big "backpack" of
dead ants

WHERE CAN YOU FIND IT?
Africa, Malaysia, and the Philippines

An ant hurries over the rocky ground. It pauses beside
a dark pebble to clean a bit of dust off its antenna. Unfortunately for the
ant, this is the last thing it will ever do. Because what looks like a pebble is
actually an assassin bug in disguise.

The bug strikes so quickly that its movements are a blur. It grabs the ant
with powerful front legs. Then it plunges its needlelike mouth into the ant's
body and injects a paralyzing poison laced with digestive juice.

The ant dies almost instantly. The bug waits a moment to give the digestive juice a chance to work. Then it sucks out the ant's liquefied insides, leaving little more than an empty shell. That empty shell might not seem like something worth keeping. But the assassin bug's table scraps are the key to its disguise.

Using its hind legs, the bug heaves the dead ant up onto its back to join at least a dozen other dead ants already there. The bodies of the deceased are all stuck together, thanks to a sticky substance that oozes from the bug's back. The assassin bug hides under this pile of dead ants, which it wears like a big, bulging backpack.

With its latest victim glued into place, the assassin bug goes back to hunting. It resumes its post beside the path that the ants are using to travel to and from their nest. No doubt another ant will be along shortly. Chances are good that it too will be fooled by the assassin bug's bizarre camouflage—and will become part of it as well.

This extreme close-up shows an assassin bug's proboscis, the mouthpart it uses to inject ants with paralyzing poison. The rounded, blue-colored structures are the bug's eyes.

Jumping spiders are skilled hunters that attack by leaping onto their prey.

The Science behind the Story

Wearing its coat of many corpses, a young *Acanthaspis petax* can easily be mistaken for something harmless. Ants—the bug's favorite prey—are very often tricked and wander within striking distance.

But does this assassin bug's disguise do double duty? Does it help the bug hide from its predators as well as its prey? Robert Jackson and Simon Pollard from the University of Canterbury in Christchurch, New Zealand, thought it might. They designed a clever experiment to find out.

Jackson and Pollard set up several glass-walled cages in their laboratory and put jumping spiders in them. Jumping spiders eat assassin bugs. "Jumping spiders were just about ideal as predators to use in these experiments," said Jackson. "They have fantastically good eyesight and are easy to raise in captivity. They are also friendly and harmless to people!"

Next, the scientists added a number of *A. petax* assassin bugs to the cages. They let some of the bugs keep their dead-ant disguises but removed the disguises from other bugs, leaving them "naked." What happened? The jumping spiders attacked the naked assassin bugs *ten times more often* than the bugs wearing disguises. "It took the spiders just a matter of minutes to recognize naked bugs as prey, since they looked like something edible rather than a confusing mound," said Pollard. This was solid evidence that using dead ants as camouflage does protect *A. petax* assassin bugs from predators—at least from jumping spiders.

And the ant disguise might not just fool predators. It might actively repel them. *A. petax* assassin bugs kill and eat several kinds of insects, but they typically stack only dead ants on their backs. Is there something special about ant corpses that make the bug's disguise more effective? "Ants are avoided by many predators," said Jackson. "They tend to be unpalatable as a meal, and they can be dangerous. Some can sting, and many have chemical defenses."

A. petax assassin bugs can carry as many as twenty dead ants on their backs at one time.

Chapter 2
COPYCAT

THE MASTER: Chick of the cinereous mourner (*Laniocera hypopyrra*), a.k.a. the Great Pretender

THE DISGUISE: Feathers and movements that mimic a furry, poisonous caterpillar

WHERE CAN YOU FIND IT? Amazon rain forests

A dull gray, robin-sized bird lands quietly on a tree branch. She has food for her hungry chick. But snakes, monkeys, and other predators roam the treetops in the rain forest.

So the mother bird waits and scans her surroundings. Insects drone in the humid air. A butterfly sails past. But nothing else seems out of place. Finally, the mother makes her move. She swoops into the leafy tangle and alights on the rim of her nest.

Her chick crouches silently in the bottom. Its bright orange feathers gleam in the sunlight. The feathers are very narrow and look like long, silky fur. Each feather has several sharp-looking orange barbs that are tipped in bright white. The chick doesn't sit up and chirp. It doesn't open its mouth for food. Instead, it begins to creep around the nest. With its strange movements and even stranger feathers, the chick doesn't look like a baby bird at all. It looks like a very big, very furry orange caterpillar.

That turns out to be the perfect disguise.

As it happens, a type of large moth also lives in the forest. When these moths are caterpillars, they are about the same size as a cinereous mourner chick. They are covered with long, silky, bright orange fur that hides sharp barbs tipped in bright white. The caterpillars crawl around, out in the open, moving their heads slowly from side to side.

Yet nothing bothers these big orange caterpillars, because touching them means getting a painful, poisonous sting.

As a cinereous mourner chick crawls around the nest, it moves its head slowly from side to side, just like the poisonous caterpillar it mimics.

The Science behind the Story

Caterpillar copycats. That is what Gustavo Londoño believes cinereous mourner chicks are. Londoño is a scientist from Icesi University in Colombia. He is also one of the few people in the world who has seen cinereous mourners and their chicks up close, in the wild.

"Back in 2001, I discovered cinereous mourners nesting at a site deep in the Peruvian rain forest where I was working on another research project," Londoño explained. Several years later, he returned to find mourners still nesting in the same area. He and his colleagues set up motion-sensor cameras near a mourner nest. "We spent only about five minutes near the nest each day because we didn't want our presence to bother the birds," he said. Triggered by the slightest movement, the cameras recorded the activities of both parents and chicks.

When the scientists studied the videos, they were struck by how closely cinereous mourner chicks resemble the big orange caterpillars they had seen crawling around the forest. Chicks and caterpillars are almost exactly the same size. They both have a

This is a photo of the poisonous rain forest caterpillar that cinereous mourner chicks so closely resemble. The caterpillars are a whopping 4.7 inches (12 centimeters) long!

furry orange body covering. They also move in very similar ways. But why would a baby bird mimic a caterpillar?

Londoño took detailed photos of the furry orange caterpillars and sent them to an insect expert. The expert determined that they were the larvae of a moth, one that belongs to the genus *Megalopyge*. A smaller but closely related moth lives in parts of the southern United States. Its caterpillars are sometimes called puss caterpillars because their long, silky fur reminds people of furry pussycats.

The caterpillars also have another nickname: tree asps. (An asp is a dangerous, poisonous snake.) That is because the caterpillars' fur conceals sharp, poison-packed spines. Like their North American counterparts, the Peruvian caterpillars have poisonous spines under their fur too.

Are cinereous mourner chicks mimicking a poisonous caterpillar to fool predators into leaving them alone? Londoño thinks they are. "The chicks and caterpillars are a very close match," he said. "Unbelievably close."

Nature offers many examples of harmless insects that mimic dangerous or poisonous insects to fool predators. Although more research is needed, cinereous mourner chicks may be the first birds known to science that have mastered the same trick.

Gustavo Londoño (*right*) and a colleague in the rain forest

Chapter 3

BABY SINGS THE BLUES

THE MASTER: Caterpillar of the Alcon large blue butterfly (*Maculinea alcon*), a.k.a. the Changeling

THE DISGUISE: Tricks ants into caring for it with scent and song

WHERE CAN YOU FIND IT?
Europe

The caterpillar takes one last

bite of the leaf. Then it lowers itself to the ground on a fine strand of silk. Now all the caterpillar needs is for a babysitter to show up.

One soon does. It's a small red ant, a worker from a nearby colony of ants. The ant inspects the caterpillar carefully, touching it gently with its antennae. The caterpillar is the same size and shape as a red ant larva. It smells like an ant larva too. The worker ant is completely fooled. It thinks the caterpillar is an ant larva far from home.

The ant carries the caterpillar back to the ant nest and down into the snug safety of the nursery. The workers there are also fooled. They "adopt" the caterpillar and treat it as if it were a real ant larva in their care. But as good as this treatment is, it's not good enough for the caterpillar. So it begins to sing.

The caterpillar's song isn't pretty. It's a scratchy, rattling cry. But it is very similar to the song that the queen ant sings. The song is so similar, in fact, that the ants in the nursery think the caterpillar is a queen ant. Whenever the caterpillar sings, the ants treat it like a queen. They surround it, protect it, and feed it the very best food.

The caterpillar keeps its babysitters fooled for nearly a year. Its ant-like scent and its queen-ant-like song guarantee continued royal treatment. Thanks to all the special care the caterpillar receives, it grows big and fat. Even when it changes from a caterpillar into a pupa inside a thin, hard case, the ants still take care of it.

The game is up, though, when the butterfly emerges from its pupal case. The butterfly exits the ant nest at top speed, with its no-longer-fooled babysitters nipping at its wings.

The top side of the wings of the Alcon large blue butterfly is blue, while the underside is tan with dark spots. Alcon large blue butterflies rely on ants to feed and care for them as caterpillars.

The Science behind the Story

Alcon large blue caterpillars can only survive to become butterflies if ants from the genus *Myrmica* take care of them. Scientists have known for some time that the caterpillars trick the ants into adopting them by secreting chemicals that make the caterpillars smell like *Myrmica* ant larvae.

More recently, scientists noticed some rather odd things taking place in ant nests that had caterpillars in their nurseries. When the nests were disturbed, ants rushed to save the caterpillars first before saving any ant larvae. When food was scarce, nursery workers fed most of what they had to the caterpillars. If food was really scarce, nursery workers actually *fed ant larvae to the caterpillars* to keep them alive!

Why were the caterpillars getting such special treatment from their babysitters?

Francesca Barbero was part of an international team of scientists that did

Francesca Barbero *(center)* and two other ant researchers in the field

experiments to find out. The scientists suspected that the ants might be making sounds. They couldn't hear anything, but they noticed that the ants often stopped and moved their bodies in a particular way. "They moved their abdomens rapidly up and down in the air," said Barbero.

To find out if the ants—and possibly the caterpillars—were making sounds, the scientists placed ants and caterpillars in a special recording chamber in their laboratory, and used tiny microphones to record any sounds being produced. They discovered that ant larvae don't make any sounds. But worker ants, queen ants, and the caterpillars definitely do.

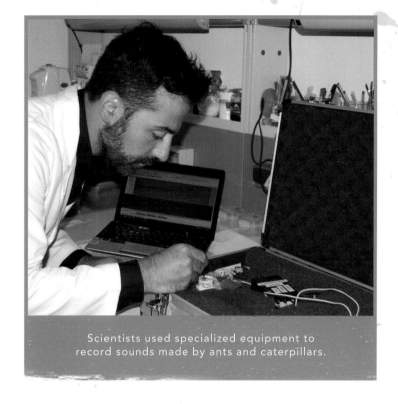

Scientists used specialized equipment to record sounds made by ants and caterpillars.

Next, the scientists played the sounds back to the ants—through very tiny speakers—and observed what happened. Playing the recorded sounds made by workers attracted the attention of workers. But playing the queen ant's sounds got the workers excited. They crowded around the speakers and wouldn't leave. When the scientists played the sounds made by the caterpillars, the worker ants behaved in much the same way.

The scientists concluded that Alcon large blue caterpillars imitate the sound that a queen ant makes. They sing the queen's "song" whenever they want special attention. "They fool ants mainly with chemistry, but they use sound when they need more care from the ants," said Barbero. By singing the queen's song, the caterpillars disguise themselves with sound as well as scent—and reap the royal benefits.

Chapter 4
YOU ARE WHAT YOU EAT

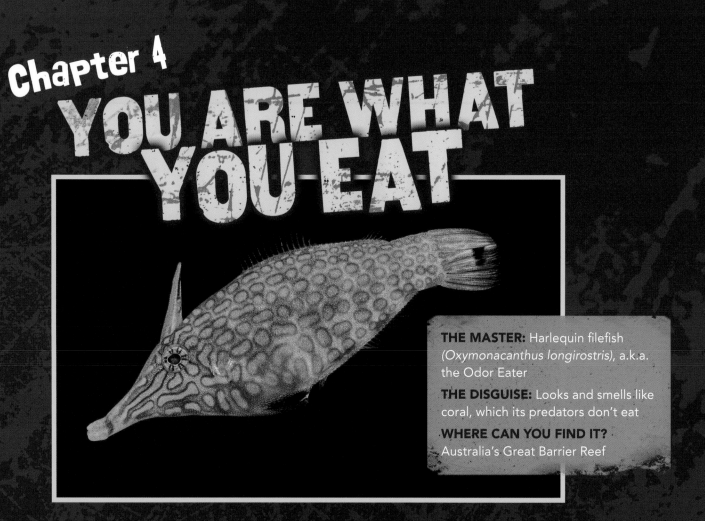

THE MASTER: Harlequin filefish (*Oxymonacanthus longirostris*), a.k.a. the Odor Eater

THE DISGUISE: Looks and smells like coral, which its predators don't eat

WHERE CAN YOU FIND IT? Australia's Great Barrier Reef

The sun sinks toward the horizon, bathing the tops of the waves in soft orange light. Beneath the waves, many animals that swim and scuttle around the coral reef during the day are going into hiding. Night brings out the hunters.

A harlequin filefish settles among the slim, spiky branches of a coral. Each branch is dotted with small bumps in which tiny coral animals, called polyps, live. The filefish's body is dotted with spots that look remarkably like the bumps on the coral.

The filefish nibbles a few polyps—a last-minute snack before bed.

These harlequin filefish swim near the coral that's both a food source and a hiding place for them.

Then the fish nestles deeper into the coral, head down among the branches. The filefish flattens its fins against its body. It folds its tail so it comes to a point. Finally, the filefish raises a hooklike spine on its head and anchors itself firmly to one coral branch.

The filefish is ready for the night ahead. It looks just like another branch of coral, complete with a pointed tip. The fish's coral-like camouflage is an effective disguise, one that will fool many sharp-eyed predators that prowl the reef at night.

Not all those predators hunt by sight alone, however. Some follow their noses to their next meal. Yet even these will likely swim right past the harlequin filefish. Why? Because the filefish doesn't just *look* like the coral in which it's hiding. It smells like the coral too.

The Science behind the Story

Rohan Brooker studies coral reef fishes. One day he read a scientific paper about a caterpillar known to take on the smell of a plant it eats. The caterpillar smells so much like the plant—and looks enough like one of its small branches—that predators typically walk right past the caterpillar without realizing it's there.

Brooker thought about harlequin filefish. They look like branches of the corals they hide in. They eat the corals too. Were filefish using the caterpillar's trick, he wondered, and further disguising themselves by smelling like the coral they eat? To find out, Brooker worked with other scientists on an island along Australia's Great Barrier Reef.

First, the scientists had to determine if harlequin filefish really do smell like the coral they eat. The scientists collected filefish from a reef near the island and divided them into two groups. For several weeks, they fed one group of filefish one type of coral and the other group a second type of coral. Next, the scientists collected two kinds of small reef crabs, some that live on the first type of coral and some that live on the second. In a series of experiments, the scientists put different combinations of crabs and filefish together in tanks. They reasoned that the crabs would be attracted to anything in the tank that smelled like their

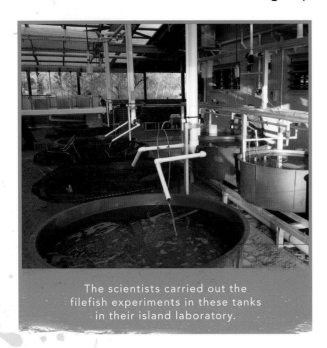

The scientists carried out the filefish experiments in these tanks in their island laboratory.

natural coral home. "The crabs appeared to have a hard time telling the difference between the smell of their favorite coral [the coral they lived on] and filefish that had eaten it," said Brooker.

This was proof that harlequin filefish do indeed take on

Coral cod inhabit coral reefs in the western Pacific and Indian Oceans. They often lurk under rocky ledges when not actively hunting smaller fish.

the odor of the coral they eat. Enough to fool crabs, at least. But are filefish predators also fooled by this coral-scented disguise? To answer this question, the scientists put coral cod, big fish that eat filefish, into tanks with different combinations of corals and filefish. (The filefish were protected inside plastic tubes. The cod couldn't see them, but they could smell them.)

When cod were put into a tank with filefish whose diet didn't match the corals in the tank, the cod actively prowled around, looking for food they could obviously smell. However, when cod were put in with filefish whose diet did match the corals in the tank, the cod seemed unaware the filefish were there. "They were pretty disinterested," Brooker said, "and spent most of their time hanging out in their shelter [on the bottom of the tank]."

The results were clear: by looking *and smelling* like coral, the harlequin filefish has a very effective antipredator disguise. It's the first fish known to do this.

Chapter 5
STRAW MAN

THE MASTER: A rain forest spider (*Cyclosa*), a.k.a. the Puppeteer

THE DISGUISE: A large, spider-shaped decoy

WHERE CAN YOU FIND IT?
Peruvian rain forests

A big spider sits motionless in the middle of its

web. A bird lands on a nearby branch. Suddenly the spider's long legs begin to twitch. Its body quivers, enough to set the whole web shaking. Alarmed, the bird flies off.

After a moment, the big spider stops moving. The delicate web grows still. Then a tiny spider crawls out from behind the big one. It moves slowly over the big spider's body, stopping here and there to make repairs.

After all that shaking, the big spider needs a bit of fixing—because it isn't really a spider at all. It's a fake. A decoy. A sort of spider puppet designed to fool passersby.

And the tiny spider built it.

The spider puppet looks very much like its maker, although it is nearly ten times larger. The puppet has eight legs, a head, and a bulging abdomen.

The tiny spider crafted its masterpiece out of bits of dead leaves, insect parts, spider egg sacs, and even some of its own shed skin. The spider carefully assembled all these materials in the shape of a big spider. It attached them to strands of silk that run through the web.

Repairs complete, the tiny spider crawls back into its hiding place. The next time something comes too close to its web, the spider will put on another performance. It will pluck the strands to make its supersized look-alike come to life and scare the threat away.

The puppet-making spider is visible directly above a much larger decoy that it is constructing.

The Science behind the Story

In 2012 scientist Phil Torres was walking through a Peruvian rain forest at night. In the beam of his flashlight, he spotted a large spider in a web beside the trail. As he leaned in for a closer look, the spider started twitching, and Torres realized he'd been tricked. He saw that the big spider was actually a collection of debris that had been cleverly assembled to look like a spider.

Perched on top of this very convincing fake was a real spider less than a quarter inch (0.6 cm) long. It was tugging on the web to make the fake spider twitch and seem to be alive.

Torres had never seen anything like this little spider and its puppet. But another scientist had. A few months earlier, Lary Reeves had discovered a different little spider in the Philippines that also assembles bits of debris in its web to create a larger-than-life spider look-alike.

Both puppet-building spiders are brand new to science. The scientists think they belong in the genus *Cyclosa*. As far as anyone knows, these newly discovered spiders are the only animals—other than people—known to create sculptures that look like themselves. "I think they make a better fake spider than I could make a fake human!" Torres said.

Torres and Reeves decided to work together and focus their research on the puppet-building spider in Peru. They have spent many hours watching and photographing these spiders

The Peruvian puppet-building spider was found in an isolated area along the Tambopata River in southeastern Peru.

in the forest, and observing how they construct their puppets. "Each piece of debris gets placed in the web and sewn in with silk," Torres explained. The scientists have also learned that maintaining spider puppets is hard work for the tiny spiders. When it rains (which happens a lot in a rain forest), the puppets are often ruined and the spiders have to rebuild them.

Phil Torres (*right*) and Lary Reeves working at night in the Peruvian rain forest

Like other web-spinning spiders, the Peruvian puppet-builder uses its web for catching food. The puppet seems to be primarily for defense. The scientists think the tiny spider may be trying to protect itself from one predator in particular: a type of damselfly that is the largest of its kind in the world. These jungle damselflies, nicknamed forest giants, deftly pluck small spiders out of their webs but steer clear of big ones. "We've no evidence—yet!" said Torres. "We're still awaiting some long term observations."

Chapter 6
DEAD RINGER

THE MASTER: Gliding lizard (*Draco cornutus*), a.k.a. the Leafy Look-Alike

THE DISGUISE: Extendable skin flaps that match the color of dead, falling leaves

WHERE CAN YOU FIND IT? Borneo in Southeast Asia

The air in the mangrove forest is hot and heavy

and tinged with the odors of salt and mud. Birds call. Insects buzz. Tiny crabs tiptoe over the roots of the mangrove trees while the tropical sun beats down on their bright green leaves.

Not all the leaves are bright green, however. Some have turned red, with splotches of dull green. These leaves are dead and will soon fall off the tree. New leaves sprouting from the branches will replace them.

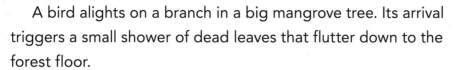

A bird alights on a branch in a big mangrove tree. Its arrival triggers a small shower of dead leaves that flutter down to the forest floor.

Every so often, a few more dead leaves fall. The bird barely glances at them—until one leaf catches its eye. This leaf is changing course halfway to the ground. It is veering toward the trunk of another tree. Too late, the bird sees that the leaf is not a leaf at all. It is a small lizard gliding through the air on outstretched flaps of skin. The scaly skin flaps are red with splotches of dull green.

The bird dives in pursuit, but the gliding lizard has a good head start. Its sharp claws grip tree bark as it lands, and in a flash, it's gone.

These gliding lizards blend in with the trees in their environment (right). When they glide from one tree to another, they extend flaps of skin (left) that enable them to closely resemble falling leaves.

The Science behind the Story

Draco cornutus is the scientific name for a group of small lizards with an unusual talent. They can glide long distances through the air on flaps of skin that they extend somewhat like wings. But as Danielle Klomp discovered on the island of Borneo, these skin flaps also work as a disguise the lizards use to fool predators.

The discovery began when Klomp and her colleagues were tramping through a mangrove forest along Borneo's coast, looking for gliding lizards in the treetops. Dead leaves occasionally fell around them, but none of the scientists paid much attention—until they noticed that some of the "leaves" were lizards. After that, Klomp said, "looking for falling leaves often revealed a lizard that had just landed on a nearby tree."

This chance observation led to another one: the red color of the gliding lizards' skin flaps matched the red color of the falling mangrove leaves. "Lots of animals use camouflage to hide from predators in conjunction with staying very still," Klomp said. But the gliding lizards "are camouflaged to match a moving part of their environment."

How effective is the leafy disguise of

Danielle Klomp holding a gliding lizard

these little lizards? Birds do catch some lizards in midair as they glide from tree to tree. But much of the time, Klomp thinks birds are fooled—at least initially. "All the lizards really need in order to evade predators," she explained, "is to trick them long enough to land on the next tree."

Scientists made another discovery about the lizards' leafy disguise when they went in search of *D. cornutus* in a forest further inland on the island. Different kinds of trees grew in the inland forest. The leaves on these trees didn't turn red when they died. Most turned a mottled green and brown.

When the scientists examined gliding lizards in this forest, they discovered that their skin flaps were also a mottled green and brown. Here was another color match between lizards

At left are the skin flaps of two different *D. cornutus* lizards. At right are dead leaves from the areas in which the lizards live.

and falling leaves. Klomp suspects that other populations of *D. cornutus* lizards, in different habitats on the island, have skin flaps that match the color of falling leaves where they live. She and her fellow scientists are planning a large research study to find out.

Chapter 7
SHELL GAME

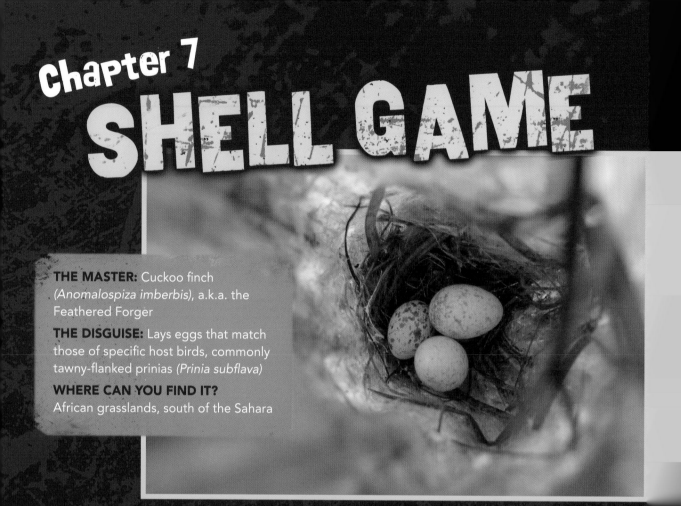

THE MASTER: Cuckoo finch
(*Anomalospiza imberbis*), a.k.a. the
Feathered Forger

THE DISGUISE: Lays eggs that match
those of specific host birds, commonly
tawny-flanked prinias (*Prinia subflava*)

WHERE CAN YOU FIND IT?
African grasslands, south of the Sahara

An African warbler called a tawny-flanked prini
has just finished laying a second egg. She leaves her nest in search of foo

A watchful cuckoo finch sees her chance. She flies to the nest and
removes one prinia egg. Then she lays an egg of her own in its place.
When the prinia returns, she doesn't spot the replacement because the
cuckoo finch's egg looks so much like hers. The two eggs are almost
exactly the same size and color, with similar spots and squiggles.

Tomorrow, when the prinia lays another egg, the cuckoo finch will like
sneak in again and pull off another egg switcheroo!

If the prinia discovered eggs in her nest that obviously looked like a stranger's, she'd toss them out in a hurry. But the cuckoo finch's eggs are nearly perfect forgeries. They resemble the prinia's eggs so closely that the prinia accepts them as her own.

Score one for the cuckoo finch. She has tricked another bird into raising some of her chicks.

The cuckoo finch's eggs will hatch a day or two before any prinia eggs. The cuckoo finch chicks will be bigger than their prinia siblings. They'll be more demanding too, which means they'll get most of the food. And they'll grow up to be con artists like their mother, duping strangers into taking care of their kids.

This cuckoo finch chick was raised by host parents and is nearly big enough to leave the nest.

The Science behind the Story

Brood parasite is the name scientists give to a bird that lays its eggs in the nests of other kinds of birds. The other birds are called hosts. A brood parasite never builds its own nest or raises its own chicks. It tricks its hosts into doing all that work.

Claire Spottiswoode studies brood parasites in Africa, including cuckoo finches. Cuckoo finches produce eggs that look astonishingly like those of their hosts, down to the smallest detail. These egg forgeries are so good, in fact, that scientists often have to look very closely to spot the difference between the forgery and the real thing.

Working with several other scientists, Spottiswoode has discovered that cuckoo finches do more than just lay eggs that are excellent imitations of their hosts' eggs. Cuckoo finches also typically lay more than one egg in each host's nest. This makes it harder for the host bird to figure out which

The eggs in the outer ring belong to tawny-flanked prinias. Eggs in the inner ring belong to cuckoo finches.

eggs are hers and which might not be. When faced with this problem, she tends to accept all the eggs in her nest rather than risk throwing out the wrong ones.

Of course, the host birds that cuckoo finches try to fool don't take all this sneakiness lying down. If a tawny-flanked prinia sees a cuckoo finch anywhere near her nest, she will attack the cuckoo finch aggressively. And if she discovers an egg in her nest that looks suspicious, she'll quickly dispose of it.

So why do cuckoo finches go to the trouble to lay eggs that mimic those of another bird? What advantage do they gain? "Raising kids is costly in terms of time and energy," Spottiswoode said. "If you can shift the cost of raising your kids onto someone else, you can have more of them!"

And in nature, having more babies means increasing the chances that your kind will survive.

A male cuckoo finch (*left*) is a much brighter shade of yellow than the female (*right*).

Chapter 8

CLOAKING DEVICE

THE MASTER: Grote's tiger moth
(*Bertholdia trigona*), a.k.a. the Bat Blaster

THE DISGUISE: Becoming "invisible" by
jamming a bat's high-frequency calls

WHERE CAN YOU FIND IT?
Southwestern United States

On a warm August night, a moth flies over the desert. It listens carefully as it flies, for there are bats on the prowl, darting through the air on leathery wings.

A burst of short, sharp, high-frequency sounds erupts out of the darkness. They are the chirping calls of a hunting bat: *CHIRP . . . CHIRP . . . CHIRP . . . CHIRP . . . CHIRP . . . CHIRP.* The sounds travel outward from the bat's mouth and strike whatever is in its path. Then the sounds bounce back, like echoes, to the bat's sensitive ears. By listening to these echoes, the bat is able to "see" very clearly what lies ahead.

The moth flies on as the bat's calls continue. Suddenly, they come much faster: *CHIRP-CHIRP-CHIRP-CHIRP-CHIRP-CHIRP-CHIRP-CHIRP-CHIRP-CHIRP-CHIRP-CHIRP*. The moth hears the change at once. It knows it has been spotted.

In moments, the bat is in hot pursuit. With a superfast *CHIRPCHIRP CHIRPCHIRPCHIRPCHIRPCHIRPCHIRPCHIRPCHIRPCHIRPCHIRP*, it locks on to the moth's position and swoops in for the kill.

A second from death, the moth takes defensive action. It dives toward the ground and, at the same time, produces a burst of its own high-frequency sounds: *click-click*.

In mid-swoop, the bat hesitates . . . and veers off. And the little moth escapes.

A brown bat approaches a tiger moth *(right)*. The inset shows a close-up of the moth's tymbal organ, which produces the high-frequency clicking sounds that allow the moth to evade bats.

The Science behind the Story

In the animal world, seeing with sound is called echolocation. It's no secret that bats are master echolocators as they fly through the night catching insect prey. Recently, Aaron Corcoran and his colleagues discovered that a small moth, called Grote's tiger moth, fights back during a bat's attack by jamming the bat's echolocation calls with sounds of its own.

There are many kinds of tiger moths. A lot of them make high-frequency clicking sounds using a special organ called a tymbal. "The clicks are barely audible to humans. If you hold a moth right up to your ear you can hear a faint rasping sound," Corcoran said.

Scientists already knew that some tiger moths click to warn predators that they are bad tasting. Others click to startle predators, creating a chance to escape. Grote's tiger moths, however, produce about ten times more clicks than any other known tiger moth species: forty-five hundred per second! Corcoran wondered if all this super-high-speed clicking was some sort of defense against bats. He carried out experiments to find out.

Corcoran's research team set up a laboratory in which bats and moths could fly around. The scientists installed microphones to record bat calls and moth clicks and cameras designed

Aaron Corcoran examines a bat.

to film in near darkness. Then they brought bats and Grote's tiger moths together and let them interact.

The bats tried to catch the moths but missed over and over again. When the scientists studied the videos and sound recordings they'd made, they found clues as to why. "Normally bats echolocate at a progressively

Scientists brought together bats and moths in this special lab and filmed them.

faster rate as they near their prey," said Corcoran. "But when a bat heard a moth's clicks, it slowed down its calling rate and then a moment later tried to speed it up again."

Corcoran and the others concluded from this response that a Grote's tiger moth's high-speed, high-frequency clicks interfere with the bat's echolocation calls. "The bat's echolocation was being jammed by the moth, and that jamming distorted the bat's perception of the moth's position."

In other words, as the bat swooped in for the kill, it suddenly wasn't able to pinpoint the moth's exact location. It's as if the moth suddenly made itself invisible, leaving the confused bat to grasp at thin air. The Grote's tiger moth is one of the few insects known to effectively jam a bat's calls.

Chapter 9

WEB OF DECEIT

THE MASTER: Assassin bug (*Stenolemus bituberus*), a.k.a. the Spider Stalker

THE DISGUISE: Creating vibrations in a spider's web that mimic a trapped insect's struggles

WHERE CAN YOU FIND IT? Australia

Tap-tap. Rap-tap-tap.

The spider feels the sudden vibrations traveling along the silken strands beneath its feet. These are the kinds of vibrations a small insect makes when it is caught in the spider's web.

Cautiously, the spider leaves the place in the web where it spends most of its time. It takes a few steps toward what it senses is the source of the vibrations and then pauses.

Rap-tap. Rap-tap.

The vibrations feel as if they are coming from something small and helpless, like an aphid or a fly. A tasty little treat that will be easy to subdue.

The spider glides closer, inching its way toward this fresh bit of dinner. *Rap. Tap. Rap.*

The spider takes another step. It tenses, ready to pounce on the meal it believes is just a body length away.

Looming above the spider is something else that's ready to pounce. It is an assassin bug—one that's quite different from the bug that wears a coat of ant corpses. This assassin bug has a talent for plucking the silken strands of a spider's web. It plucks them in just the right way to lure the spider to its death.

In one swift movement, the assassin bug strikes and the spider becomes the meal.

The Science behind the Story

With its spindly legs and sliver-thin body, the spider-stalking assassin bug *Stenolemus bituberus* looks almost too fragile to be deadly. But it is a master of deception. The bug creeps stealthily into the web of a spider. Then it tricks the spider into coming within striking distance by plucking the web's silken strands in a way that mimics the struggles of small, trapped insects. Unlike jumping spiders, most web-building spiders have very poor eyesight, so they sense what is caught in their webs by the vibrations it creates.

Anne Wignall from Massey University in New Zealand studies many kinds of insects, including *S. bituberus*. Along with several other scientists, she set out to investigate just how this assassin bug manages to fool its spider prey so well. In their laboratory, the scientists placed web-building spiders from the genus *Achaearanea* in wooden frames and let them spin their webs. Along with video cameras, they set up laser instruments that could detect and record the tiniest vibrations moving along the webs' silken strands. "Spider silk is excellent at transmitting vibrations," Wignall said.

The researchers then dropped or gently tossed different items into the webs: bits of leaves, tiny flies, and so forth. They recorded the vibrations each object or insect made and then filmed the spiders' reactions.

Then the scientists introduced the assassin bugs. Each bug approached a web, tapping and plucking the web's fine strands with its front feet. The vibration-measuring instruments showed that the bug created vibrations very similar to those made by a small insect that was firmly caught and getting tired from its struggles. "The bug plucks the silk in order to generate the types of vibrations that mimic prey in the web," Wignall explained.

These kinds of vibrations caused the spider to approach relatively slowly, which gave the assassin bug time to position itself in just the right way so it could take the spider by surprise. A surprise attack is important, because stalking a spider is risky business. The scientists witnessed a few assassin bugs whose attacks went wrong, and they ended up being eaten by the spiders they'd been hunting!

Anne Wignall in Australia's Kosciuszko National Park

Afterword
HOW DO THEY DO IT?

You may be wondering how all these masters of disguise are able to do what they do. These animals don't think about, or consciously figure out, their disguises. They don't decide to mimic eggs, work to learn an ant song, or choose to look like a poisonous caterpillar. They look and act the way they do automatically and instinctively, thanks to a remarkable set of instructions each one carries inside its cells.

This set of instructions is the genetic material known as deoxyribonucleic acid (DNA). The individual instructions that make up DNA are called genes. Genes control the characteristics, or traits, of all living things. Parents pass on their genes and, therefore, their traits to their offspring.

In any population of living things, the individuals that typically survive long enough to reproduce are those whose traits give them some sort of advantage. Having a good disguise can be a big advantage when it comes to survival. As a result, good disguises tend to be passed on—and fine-tuned—generation after generation. Over long periods of time, truly astonishing disguises are produced by this evolutionary process.

Take A. *petax* as an example. Scientists know of other assassin bugs that put dirt and bits of debris on their backs as camouflage. So perhaps the A. *petax* story unfolded something like this: A long, long time ago, a few assassin bugs occasionally heaved a dead ant onto their back, in addition to dirt and debris. Doing so gave them an advantage that increased their chances of survival. When these bugs reproduced, they passed on their dead-ant-collecting tendency—coded in their genes—to their offspring. Over time, some bugs stacked several dead ants on their backs, which gave them an even better chance of surviving. They passed this tendency on to their descendants. This continued, generation after countless generation, until the assassin bugs we know as *A. petax*, which pile their backs high with lots of dead ants, came into existence.

Scientists will never know all the details as to how such masters of disguise evolved. But they are having great success—and a lot of fun—figuring out how these remarkable animals pull off the amazing tricks they perform in the endless struggle to survive.

MEET THE SCIENTISTS

Francesca Barbero
University of Turin
Turin, Italy

Rohan Brooker
University of Delaware
Newark, Delaware

Aaron Corcoran
Wake Forest University
Winston-Salem,
North Carolina

Robert Jackson
University of Canterbury
Christchurch,
New Zealand

Danielle Klomp
University of New South
Wales
Sydney, Australia

Gustavo Londoño
Icesi University
Cali, Colombia

Simon Pollard
University of Canterbury
Christchurch,
New Zealand

Claire Spottiswoode
University of Cape Town
Cape Town, South Africa

Phil Torres
Science correspondent,
Al Jazeera America

Anne E. Wignall
Massey University
Auckland, New Zealand

SOURCE NOTES

8 Robert Jackson, e-mail communication with the author, July 10, 2015.

9 Simon Pollard, e-mail communication with the author, August 2, 2015.

9 Jackson, e-mail.

12 Gustavo Londoño, e-mail communication with the author, June 25, 2015.

12 Ibid.

13 Ibid.

16 Francesca Barbero, e-mail communication with the author, August 3, 2015.

17 Ibid.

21 Rohan Brooker, e-mail communication with the author, July 2, 2015.

21 Ibid.

24 Phil Torres, e-mail communication with the author, September 4, 2015.

25 Ibid.

25 Ibid.

28 Danielle Klomp, e-mail communication with the author, July 1, 2015.

28 Ibid.

29 Ibid.

33 Claire Spottiswoode, e-mail communication with the author, July 27, 2015.

36 Aaron Corcoran, e-mail communication with the author, June 29, 2015.

37 Ibid.

37 Ibid.

40 Anne Wignall, e-mail communication with the author, June 24, 2015.

40 Ibid.

GLOSSARY

assassin: a living thing that uses a surprise attack to catch its prey

brood: baby birds that hatched together

camouflage: disguise that helps an animal blend in with its surroundings

cinereous: an ashy-gray color

cloaking device: a method of disguise that makes something seem to be invisible

corpse: dead body

dead ringer: something that looks exactly like something else

debris: small pieces, typically of something that has been broken down or destroyed

decoy: an imitation of something that can fool or mislead

echolocation: a method for locating prey that involves producing sounds and listening for the returning echoes. It is used by bats, dolphins, and some other animals.

forgery: a copy

genus: in science, a group of related organisms that share certain characteristics. A genus is made up of one or more species.

larva: the young, wormlike feeding form of many insects that hatches from an egg and later changes into the adult form

mimic: to imitate

parasite: an organism that lives in or on another organism called the host and gains food or protection from it without offering anything in return

predator: an animal that captures and eats other animals

prey: an animal that is captured and eaten by predators

shell game: a sneaky trick that fools or confuses onlookers

species: a specific type, or kind, of organism

straw man: like a scarecrow, an imitation or dummy used to scare something away

toxic: poisonous

vibration: a series of small, rapid back-and-forth or up-and-down movements

SELECTED BIBLIOGRAPHY

Barbero, F., J. A. Thomas, S. Bonelli, E. Balletto, and K. Schönrogge. "Queen Ants Make Distinctive Sounds That Are Mimicked by a Butterfly Social Parasite." *Science* 323, no. 5915 (February 6, 2009): 782–785. doi:10.1126/science.1163583.

Brooker, Rohan M., Philip L. Munday, Douglas P. Chivers, and Geoffrey P. Jones. "You Are What You Eat: Diet-Induced Chemical Crypsis in a Coral-Feeding Reef Fish." *Proceedings of the Royal Society B* 282, no. 1799 (January 2015). http://dx.doi.org/10.1098/rspb.2014.1887.

Corcoran, Aaron J., Jesse R. Barber, and William E. Conner. "Tiger Moth Jams Bat Sonar." *Science* 325, no. 5938 (July 17, 2009): 325–327. doi:10.1126/science.1174096.

Drake, Nadia. "Spider That Builds Its Own Spider Decoys Discovered." *Wired*, December 18, 2012. http://www.wired.com/2012/12/spider-building-spider/.

Jackson, R. R., and S. D. Pollard. "Bugs with Backpacks Deter Vision-Guided Predation by Jumping Spiders." *Journal of Zoology* 273, no. 4 (December 2007): 358–363. doi:10.1111/j.1469-7998.2007.00335.x.

Klomp, D. A., D. Stuart-Fox, I. Das, and T. J. Ord. "Marked Colour Divergence in the Gliding Membranes of a Tropical Lizard Mirrors Population Differences in the Colour of Falling Leaves." *Royal Society Biology Letters* 10, no. 12 (December 24, 2014). doi:10.1098/rsbl.2014.0776.

Londoño, Gustavo A., Duván A. García, and Manuel A. Sánchez Martínez. "Morphological and Behavioral Evidence of Batesian Mimicry in Nestlings of a Lowland Amazonian Bird." *American Naturalist* 185, no. 1 (January 2015): 135–141.

Stevens, Martin, Jolyon Troscianko, and Claire N. Spottiswoode. "Repeated Targeting of the Same Hosts by a Brood Parasite Compromises Host Egg Rejection." *Nature Communications* 4, no. 2475 (September 24, 2013). doi:10.1038/ncomms3475.

Torres, Phil. "New Species of 'Decoy' Spider Likely Discovered at Tambopata Research Center." *Peru Nature Blog*, December 10, 2012. http://blog.perunature.com/2012/12/new-species-of-decoy-spider-likely.html.

Wignall, A. E., and P. W. Taylor. "Assassin Bug Uses Aggressive Mimicry to Lure Spider Prey." *Proceedings of the Royal Society B, Biological Sciences* 278, no. 1710 (May 2011): 1427–1433. doi:10.1098/rspb.2010.2060.

MORE TO EXPLORE

Books

Johnson, Rebecca L. *When Lunch Fights Back: Wickedly Clever Animal Defenses*. Minneapolis: Millbrook Press, 2015.

———. *Zombie Makers: True Stories of Nature's Undead*. Minneapolis: Millbrook Press, 2013.

Riehecky, Janet. *Camouflage and Mimicry: Animal Weapons and Defenses*. Mankato, MN: Capstone, 2012.

Wilsdon, Christina. *Animal Defenses*. New York: Chelsea House, 2009.

Websites

African Cuckoos
  http://www2.zoo.cam.ac.uk/africancuckoos/systems/cuckoofinch.html
  Find out more about cuckoo finches and the latest research on these birds.

Gliding Lizards Mimic Falling Leaves
  http://www.anoleannals.org/2015/01/17/gliding-lizards-mimic-falling-leaves/
  This blog post by Danielle Klomp offers more details about how the scientists studying gliding lizards developed their falling leaves hypothesis.

SonarJamming.com
  http://www.sonarjamming.com/
  Scientist Aaron Corcoran created this site, which includes information about moths that jam bat sonar as well as photos and videos.

Terrestrial Camouflage
  http://sensoryecology.com/research-themes/terrestrial-camouflage.html
  This site from a group of scientists has a section describing current research projects related to animal camouflage.

Videos

Amazonian Bird Chicks Mimic Poisonous Caterpillar to Avoid Detection
  http://phys.org/news/2014-12-amazonian-bird-chicks-mimic-poisonous.html
  See how a cinereous mourner chick imitates a caterpillar's movements.

Ant-Killing Assassin Bugs (*Acanthaspis petax*), Bukidnon, Philippines
https://www.youtube.com/watch?v=l0dScmH8c5U
Watch several *A. petax* assassin bugs wearing their backpacks of ant corpses.

Assassin Bugs Trap Spiders by Mimicking Prey
http://phys.org/news/2010-10-assassin-bugs-spiders-mimicking-prey.html
Watch a short clip of assassin bug *S. bituberus* luring and attacking a spider.

First Video of New Spider Species!
https://www.youtube.com/watch?v=RrWnZ7VySac
View the first video footage of Phil Torres and other researchers observing the Peruvian puppet-building spider at night in the rain forest.

Nat Geo: Moth Jamming Bat
http://www.sonarjamming.com/apps/videos/videos/show/18209271-nat-geo-moth -jamming-bat
This clip from National Geographic *Untamed Americas* program shows tiger moths successfully evading bats.

Secrets of Animal Camouflage Research
https://www.youtube.com/watch?v=JGd9hl5X20Q&feature=iv&src_vid=7JzELgqdicQ &annotation_id=annotation_1847847419
Jolyon Troscianko describes research he's conducting with several other scientists into how camouflage works.

INDEX

PHOTO ACKNOWLEDGMENTS

The images in this book are used with the permission of: © Tane Sinclair-Taylor, pp. 1, 19 © Parfta/ Deposit Photos, p. 4 (Fern leaf) © Johann Schumacher/Photolibrary RM/Getty Images, p. 5; © Hock Ping GUEK/Kurt, pp. 6, 9, 42; © Albert Lleal/Minden Pictures, p. 7; © Eran Finkle/Wikimedia Commons (CC BY-SA 3.0), p. 8; © Gustavo Adolfo Londoño, PhD/Profesor, Universidad ICESI/Cali-Colombia, pp. 10, 11, 12, 13, 43 (portrait); Courtesy of Francesca Barbero, pp. 14, 15, 16, 17, 43 (portrait); © Paul Starosta/ Corbis, p. 18; Courtesy of Rohan Brooker, pp. 20, 43 (portrait); © David Fleetham/naturepl.com, p. 21; © Lary Reeves/Phil Torres, pp. 22, 23, 24, 25, 43 (bottom left); © Ch'ien Lee/Minden Pictures, p. 26; © Devi Stuart-Fox, p. 27 (both); © Danielle Klomp, pp. 28, 29, 43 (portrait) © Dr. Claire N. Spottiswoode, pp. 30, 31, 32, 33 (all), 43 (portrait); Courtesy of Dr. Aaron Corcoran, pp. 34, 35 (all), 36, 37, 43 (portrait); © Dr. Anne E. Wignall, p. 38; © Aaron Harmer, pp. 40, 43 (bottom right); Courtesy of Robert Jackson, p. 43 (top right); Courtesy of Simon Pollard, p. 43 (second row middle right).

Front cover: © Liewwk/Dreamstime.com.

Back cover: © Parfta/Deposit Photos.